A Guide for Using

Curious George

and Other
Curious George Books

in the Classroom

Based on the book written by H. A. Rey

This guide written by **Mary Bolte**

Teacher Created Resources, Inc.
6421 Industry Way
Westminster, CA 92683
www.teachercreated.com

©2001 Teacher Created Resources, Inc.
Reprinted, 2006

Made in U.S.A.

ISBN 0-7439-3152-1

Edited by
Lorin Klistoff, M.A.

Illustrated by
Wendy Chang

Cover Art by
Wendy Chang

Table of Contents

Introduction

Curious, inquisitive, clever, inventive, and original. These words describe George, a captivating little monkey who was taken many years ago from his native land, Africa, by the man in the yellow hat, to live in a new land. Since then, George has been an inspiration to his readers and fans, who have learned to actively pursue and accept life's challenges.

George remains under the care of the man in the yellow hat in the original, first seven books in the Curious George series. This unit includes activities for the seven books, beginning with his arrival in a new land and a new home in the zoo and ending with the seventh book, which is entertaining and educational as readers become more familiar with hospital life. After sharing one of the other Curious George books with the class, refer to the Appendix (pages 46–47) for suggested activities.

The Be Curious! activities following the unit activities are related extensions to encourage and motivate the readers to be curious and explore new directions.

A Sample Lesson Plan

The Sample Lesson Plan on page 4 provides you with a set of introductory lesson-plan suggestions for the first book in the series, *Curious George*, which introduce George and the man in the yellow hat to the reader. Each of the lessons can take from one to several days and may include all or some of the suggested activities. Refer to the Suggestions for Using the Unit Activities on pages 7–10 for information relating to the unit activities.

A Unit Planner

If you wish to tailor the suggestions on pages 7–10 to a format other than the one described in the Sample Lesson Plan, a blank Unit Planner is provided on page 5. Plan each day on this planner sheet by writing the activities or brief notations about the lessons that you wish to accomplish. Space has been provided for reminders, comments, and other pertinent information related to each day's activities. Reproduce copies of the Unit Planner as needed.

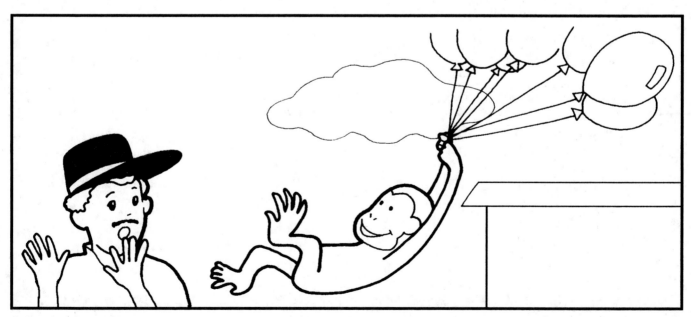

Sample Lesson Plan

Lesson 1

- Read Getting to Know the Books and the Authors on page 6 with your students.
- Do Before the Book activities 2, 3, 4, 5, and 6 on page 7.
- Read the story for enjoyment.

Lesson 2

- Introduce the vocabulary on page 8 and complete the Into the Book activity 1.
- Reread the story listening for the vocabulary words.
- Retell the story using A Story Retell activity on page 21.
- Complete The Seven Continents activity on page 33.
- Design and write about hats and caps on page 41.

Lesson 3

- Complete Into the Book activity 2 on page 8, using the questions on page 14.
- Explore fire trucks and fire engines.
- Complete the Fire Trucks, Fire Engines activity on page 28.
- Discuss the dangers of smoking.
- Complete the activity, No Smoking, Please! on page 36.
- Share pictures, ads, etc., of different kinds of telephones. Then complete Telephones on page 29.

Lesson 4

- Read *Curious George Goes to the Hospital* and emphasize George's puppet show in the playroom. In groups, practice reading the Readers Theater script on pages 43 and 44.
- Discuss the five senses. Then read the rhymes and complete the Rhymes Make Sense! activity on page 24.
- Share ideas about being curious and wondering. Complete Did You Ever Wonder? on page 23 and share stories.
- Together, read, complete, and practice the song, Let's Follow George!, on pages 31 and 32.
- Complete A Bunch of Balloons! on page 27.

Lesson 5

- Continue to practice the Readers Theater script, the rhymes, and the Let's Follow George! song.
- Work in groups to make the stick puppets and theaters on pages 18, 19, and 20.
- Treat the students to a banana snack. Read about the healthy benefits of bananas on page 37 and then complete the activity.
- Share other kinds of fruit and discuss how they are grown. Complete the Fruit! Fruit! activity on page 38.

Lesson 6

- In groups, practice the Readers Theater scripts using the stick puppets and theaters.
- Practice the rhymes and the Let's Follow George! song.
- Culmination: Before an audience, perform the Readers Theater puppet presentation, the rhymes, and song.

Unit Planner

Unit Activities	Unit Activities
Date:	Date:
Notes:	Notes:
Unit Activities	Unit Activities
Date:	Date:
Notes:	Notes:
Unit Activities	Unit Activities
Date:	Date:
Notes:	Notes:

Getting to Know the Books and the Authors

About the Books

George first appeared in Paris, as one of nine monkeys in the book, *Cecily G. and the Nine Monkeys*. In 1941, he was introduced to America in the book, *Curious George*. George continued to be a favorite of enthusiastic readers as they compared him to their own lives. His unique, yet realistic adventures, at times, caused trouble, but resulted in some value which was always recognized. Each book displays this theme, as readers are stimulated to believe in themselves and recognize the positive accomplishments in their daily-life experiences.

The seven books in this series should motivate curious readers to discover other adapted George books that offer new, everyday life experiences that will be enjoyed by all.

About the Authors

Hans and Margret Rey were both born in Hamburg, Germany—Hans Augusto (H. A.) on September 16, 1898, and Margret on May 16, 1906. At a young age, Hans had a talent in art which developed into a full-time profession after he met and married Margret, who was mainly a writer. They collaborated in the publication of many children's books. Margret usually did the writing and H. A. the illustrating.

They were married in 1935 in Rio de Janeiro, Brazil, to escape Nazi Germany. Later they moved to Paris, where they published their first book together, *Cecily G. and the Nine Monkeys*, with George being one of the "nine."

In June, 1940, before the Nazis entered Paris— with warm clothes on their backs and their manuscripts, which included George as one of the characters—H. A. and Margret rode their bicycles to the French-Spanish border, sold them, and took the train to Lisbon, Spain. Soon thereafter they returned to Rio de Janeiro before immigrating to the U.S.A. in 1940.

A week later, they sold their Curious George idea to the Houghton Mifflin Company. The rest of their lives were devoted to writing children's picture books and sharing life's adventures through the Curious George Series.

H. A. died in 1977 and Margret died in 1996. They will always be remembered for the clever and curious little monkey named George and the man in the yellow hat, who change this little monkey's life.

Suggestions for Using the Unit Activities

Use some or all of the suggestions to introduce your students to George in *Curious George* and to extend their appreciation of the book through activities that cross the curriculum. Activities for the other six books in the series are explained in the Appendix. The suggested activities for *Curious George* have been divided into three sections to assist you in the planning of this unit.

The sections are arranged as follows:

Before the Book: includes suggestions for preparing the classroom environment and the students for the literature to be read.

Into the Book: has activities that focus on the book's content, characters, theme, etc., and the "Be Curious!" extended activities.

After the Book: extends the readers' enjoyment of the book.

Before the Book

1. Before you begin the unit, prepare the vocabulary cards, story questions, and sentence strips for the pocket chart activities. (See the Into the Book section on page 8 and the Story Questions on page 14.)

2. Display and share the different Curious George books in this unit. Research information about monkeys and discuss the different kinds of monkeys, their characteristics and habitats.

3. Read the information about the author H. A. Rey and his wife, Margret Rey, on page 6.

4. Set the stage for reading the books by discussing the following questions: What does it mean to be curious? Who can be curious? Why do humans and animals become curious? What may happen when one becomes curious? Have you ever been curious? What happened?

5. Display the cover of the book. Ask the following questions about the cover:

   • What is happening to George?
   • How do you know that?
   • Why does one firefighter have a telephone?
   • Why is one firefighter pointing?
   • Where do you think they are going?
   • How does George feel about walking with the firefighters?
   • How do you know that?

6. Introduce the other characters in the book: the man with the big, yellow hat; the sailors; the firefighters; and the balloon man.

Suggestions for Using the Unit Activities *(cont.)*

Into the Book

Language Arts

1. **Pocket Chart Activity: Vocabulary Cards**

   After reading the book, discuss the meaning of the following words in context. Make copies of the monkey on page 13. Write the words on the monkeys and the definitions on sentence strips. Display the monkeys in a pocket chart. Have students match the definitions with the vocabulary words. (See page 11.)

Vocabulary Words			
Africa	curious	fascinated	trouble
yellow	naughty	promised	fire station
sailor	forget	prison	frightened

2. **Pocket Chart Activity: Story Questions**

   Develop critical thinking skills, using the story questions on page 14. The questions are based on Bloom's taxonomy and are provided for each level of Bloom's Levels of Learning. Reproduce the hat pattern on page 13. Write each question on a hat and place them in the pocket chart. Then discuss each question.

3. **More Pocket Chart Activities**

   • Brainstorm a list of sentences retelling the important parts of the book. Display them in the pocket chart out of order. Have students put the sentences in the order in which the events happened in the story.

   • Write each of George's problems on a sentence strip. Then discuss how each problem was solved.

   • Put quotations from the story on sentence strips. Print the name or names of the speakers on separate cards. Use them for a matching activity on the pocket chart.

4. **A Story Retell** (page 21)

   Discuss the directions. Complete directions one and two together or independently. Students may complete direction three with classmates.

5. **Curious George or Bored George?** (page 22)

   Brainstorm lists of antonyms and synonyms. Discuss the directions and have each student complete the activity individually and then share the sentences and questions with classmates.

Suggestions for Using the Unit Activities *(cont.)*

Into the Book *(cont.)*

Language Arts *(cont.)*

6. **Did You Ever Wonder?** (page 23)

   Students share thoughts about the word *wonder* and how it is similar to the word *curious*. Review the five senses and how they effect our everyday lives. Then complete the written activity independently.

7. **Rhymes Make Sense!** (page 24)

   Brainstorm words with similar word endings and create short rhymes using the words. Discuss the directions, exploring how the five senses, daily, influenced George. Complete the activity together or independently.

8. **A New Curious George Tale!** (page 25)

   After students have read the story, they can create a new beginning to the *Curious George* book.

Math

1. **A Bunch of Balloons!** (page 27)

   Discuss the directions. Have students individually complete the problems and then the Be Curious! activity. Culminate the activity with the children sharing their solutions for the two "mysterious balloons."

2. **Fire Trucks, Fire Engines** (page 28)

   Share information about fire-fighting equipment and discuss the number and sets of tires on different kinds of trucks and cars. If possible, visit a fire station and learn about its operation. Together, read the descriptions of the different cars and trucks seen in a fire station. Students then complete the activity.

3. **Telephones** (page 29)

   Discuss the importance of the telephone, different kinds of telephones, and telephone numbers. Review the mathematical terms used when explaining addition (*addends, sum, add, plus, equals,* etc.) and subtraction (*subtrahend, minuend, subtract, take away, difference, equals,* etc.). Then complete the activity independently and share solutions.

4. **Let's Follow George!** (pages 31 and 32)

   Together sing "Mary Had a Little Lamb" to familiarize students with the tune. Then sing the first two verses together and complete the next five verses using words that link the five senses to the different places visited. This song can also be written and then acted out as students pretend or actually walk to the different places. They can take turns being the leader, George.

Suggestions for Using the Unit Activities *(cont.)*

Into the Book *(cont.)*

Social Studies

1. **The Seven Continents** (page 33)

   Review and locate the seven continents and the oceans of the world, emphasizing Africa. Students then complete the map activity independently.

Health

1. **No Smoking, Please!** (page 36)

   Discuss the dangers of smoking. Begin a campaign to encourage people not to smoke. Brainstorm different slogans. Students then design signs showing the slogan.

2. **Bananas! Bananas!** (page 37)

   Read and discuss the story about bananas. Students write and share a paragraph detailing what they learned about bananas.

Science

1. **Fruit! Fruit!** (page 38)

   Research different kinds of fruit and how they grow. Discuss the directions and complete the activity independently. Share the results and list the different fruits for each of the four groups.

Art

1. **Hats and Caps** (page 41)

   Have a hat-and-cap day. Students share their favorite hat and/or caps and then complete the activity. Make a book displaying the hats, caps, and paragraphs.

After the Book: Culminating Activity

1. **Readers Theater Script** (pages 43 and 44)

   Read *Curious George Goes to the Hospital* and talk about the puppet show he performed for the children. Assemble the students into groups of seven and provide each with a copy of the script. Highlight the parts and laminate the scripts before distributing them. The groups practice reading the script together. Then prepare the puppets for the sailor, fireman, balloon man, and policeman on pages 19 and 20. Each narrator makes a "George" puppet. To create puppet theaters, refer to the directions on page 18. Use larger, appliance boxes to make bigger puppet theaters. When the groups are ready to perform, invite others to attend.

Pocket Chart Activities

Prepare a pocket chart for storing and using the vocabulary cards, the question cards, and the sentence strips.

How to Make a Pocket Chart

If a commercial pocket chart is unavailable, you can make a pocket chart if you have access to a laminator. Begin by laminating a 24" x 36" (61 cm x 91 cm) piece of colored tagboard. Cut nine 2" x 20" (5 cm x 51 cm) or six 3" x 20" (8 cm x 51 cm) strips of clear plastic to use as pockets. Space the strips equally down the 36" (91 cm) length of the tagboard. Attach each strip with clear, plastic tape along the sides and bottom. This will hold the sentence strips, word cards, etc., and can be displayed in the learning center or mounted on a chalk tray for use with a group. When your pocket chart is ready, use it to display sentence strips, vocabulary and question cards.

How to Use a Pocket Chart

1. On brown, light-brown, or tan paper, reproduce the monkey pattern on page 13. Copy each vocabulary word found on page 8 on a monkey. Write the corresponding definition for each word on a sentence strip. Have students match each vocabulary word to the correct definition. When a match has been made, place the word and the sentence strip next to each other in the pocket chart. (See illustration below.)

2. Summarize the story in several sentences. This can either be done in advance by the teacher or by the students. (The events on page 21, A Story Retell, can be copied.) Write each sentence on a sentence strip. Each student can then work alone or with a partner at a learning center to practice sequencing the sentence strips. As an extension, have students create their own minibooks by copying the sentences on sheets of paper stapled together. They can then illustrate each page.

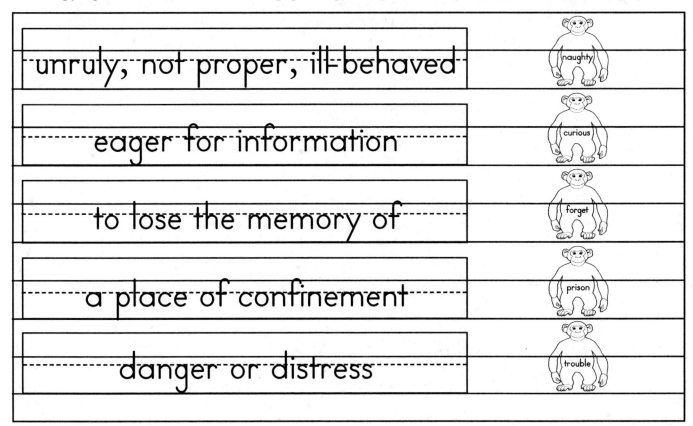

Pocket Chart Activities *(cont.)*

How to Use a Pocket Chart *(cont.)*

3. Reproduce several copies of the hat pattern on page 13 in six different colors. Write a story question from page 14 on each hat pattern. The level of the question can be written on the hat, too. If you desire, laminate each piece for durability. Use a different color of paper for each level of Bloom's Levels of Learning.

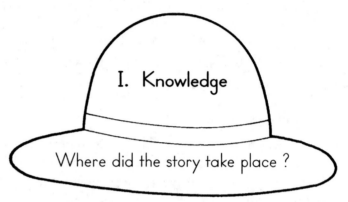

    I. Knowledge *(red)*

    II. Comprehension *(orange)*

    III. Application *(yellow)*

    IV. Analysis *(green)*

    V. Synthesis *(blue)*

    VI. Evaluation *(purple)*

Use the hat cards after reading the story. These will provide opportunities for the students to develop and practice higher-level critical thinking skills.

- Play a game. Divide the class into teams. Ask for a response to a question from one of the question cards. You may choose to have a student select a card and read it aloud or give it to the teacher to read aloud. Have the student answer the question or call on a volunteer to answer. Teams score a point for each appropriate response. If the questions have been prepared for several different Curious George books, mix up the cards and ask the team members to respond by also naming the book that relates to the question. Award extra points for this information.

- Arrange students in pairs. Read the questions and ask the partners to take turns answering them.

Pocket Chart Patterns

Directions: Duplicate these patterns, as needed, for use with the pocket chart activities on pages 11 and 12. Enlarge or reproduce the pattern to fit a particular activity.

Story Questions

Use the following questions based on Bloom's Levels of Learning to develop higher-level, critical thinking skills. The levels are as follows: **I. Knowledge** (*ability to recall learned information*), **II. Comprehension** (*ability to master basic understanding of information*), **III. Application** (*ability to do something new with information*), **IV. Analysis** (*ability to examine the parts of a whole*), **V. Synthesis** (*ability to bring together information to make something new*), and **VI. Evaluation** (*ability to form and defend an opinion*). The questions promote discussion and provide excellent reasons for returning to the text to review the story.

Reproduce the hat (page 13) as directed on page 12. Write a different question from Bloom's Levels of Learning on each of the hats. Use the hats with the suggested activities.

Curious George
I. Who is George? Who were the other characters? Where did the story take place? Where and why did the man with the big, yellow hat take George? What happened when George went to live with him?
II. What happened when George became curious on the ship? When he discovered the telephone? When he was put in prison? When he saw the balloon man? How did the man with the big, yellow hat help George?
III. What might have happened if George was not curious? If he had not put on the large, yellow hat? If the rowboat had not found the big ship?
IV. Why do you think the man with the big, yellow hat always helped George? Do you think George and the man respected each other? Why? What do you think George learned from all his experiences?
V. How might this story have changed if George had flown in an airplane across the ocean? If George stayed out of trouble? If George could talk?
VI. Why do you think George and the man with the big, yellow hat were the best of friends? If you were the man, would you always help George with his problems? Why? Are you ready to read another book about George? Why?

Curious George Takes a Job
I. Why did George want to leave the Zoo? How did George get out of the Zoo? What did he do after he got out of the Zoo?
II. How did curiosity help George learn more about the city? How did it get him in trouble? What happened when George tried different jobs in the city? How did his friend with the big, yellow hat help him?
III. What might have happened if George had explored the Zoo instead of the city? If George had taken the elevator to escape, what might have happened? Do you think George will be curious again? Why?
IV. Why do you think George stayed out of trouble when filming his movie? Do you think all of the city workers reacted to George in the right way? Why? What do you think George learned from his experience in the city?
V. How would the story have ended if the man with the big, yellow hat had not bought a newspaper? In the hospital, what would have happened if George had played with the cotton and bandages instead of the ether? What do you think George will do the next time he is curious in the city?
VI. If you were George, would you leave your home in the Zoo? George is always curious. Is this a good habit? Why? If you were the man with the big, yellow hat, would you always come to George's rescue? Why?

Story Questions *(cont.)*

Curious George Rides a Bike

I. Why did the man with the big, yellow hat give George a bike? Where did George go with his bicycle? What did George do with his newspapers? Who helped George, and what happened?

II. Why was the bicycle important in the story? How did George's curiosity help him to help others in the story? How did the other characters in the story show their respect for George?

III. What might have happened if the bicycle was a unicycle? If each newspaper was in a plastic bag, what may have happened? How would the story have changed if George had made airplanes out of the newspapers?

IV. Do you think the man with the yellow hat was right in giving George a bicycle? Why? Why do you think George left the newsboy? What do you think George learned from this experience?

V. What would have happened if George had kept delivering all of the newspapers? How would the story have changed if George had seen birds instead of ducks? How might the story have changed if George had a cell phone?

Curious George Gets a Medal

I. What started all of George's problems? Where did he find all the things he needed to try to solve his "ink" problem? Why and where did George hide in the story? Why did George get a medal?

II. What were the different problems George had in the story? How did he solve them? How did the man with the yellow hat help George? Why was George forgiven for the trouble he caused?

III. What might have happened if George had found a pencil instead of a pen without ink? How would the story have changed if the man with the yellow hat had been at home to read the letter to George? Do you think George will hide again if he has a problem? Why?

IV. Why do you think George's ideas to clean up his messes became a big problem? What do you think was George's best decision in the story? Why? Do you think George was happy about his space trip? Why?

V. How would the story have ended if George got lost in space? What would have happened if George's parachute had landed on a banana tree in Africa? How did George's curiosity help him to solve one problem, but cause another? What do you think George's next adventure will be?

VI. If you were the man with the yellow hat, would you leave George alone for more than 20 minutes? Why? Do you think George knew the difference between real and unreal? Why? If you were George, would you have tried to solve his problems in the same way? Why?

Story Questions *(cont.)*

Curious George Flies a Kite

I. Why did George want to go to the little house in the big garden? What happened when George played with the baby bunny? What happened when George went fishing? What happened when George and Bill flew the kite? Why was George happy at the end of the story?

II. In what way were the beginning and the ending of the story alike? How did string play an important part in George's adventures? Who were George's friends in the story, and how did they help him? At the end of the story, what made George think about being curious again?

III. What might have happened if a dog was in the little house? If George had used bananas for bait, what might have happened? How would you have watched Bill's kite? Do you think George will go into a strange house again? Why?

IV. How did George's curiosity get him in and out of trouble? What was George's best idea in the story? Why? Why do you think Bill gave George a baby bunny?

V. How might the story have changed if Bill had found string in the garden? What do you think George will do the next time he is curious?

VI. How do you think George will treat the baby bunny? Why? Is "Get the Bunny" a good game to play with an animal? Why? If you were fishing and caught no fish, would you try to catch them with your hands? Why? Is it always best to do as you are told? Why?

Curious George Learns the Alphabet

I. Why did the man with the yellow hat want George to learn the alphabet? How did the man teach George each letter? What words did George learn to read or write?

II. Why did George learn the letters easily? Why did the man with the yellow hat teach the letters in small groups instead of 26 at one time? At the end, how did you know that George had learned to read?

III. What might have happened if the man had taught the alphabet with no pictures or words? Do you think George will read and write words every day? Why? How would you have taught George to read and write words and letters?

IV. Do you think the picture letters were meaningful to George? Why? Why did the man stop at 13 letters and have George write words? What were some of the more meaningful words the man used when teaching the alphabet?

V. What might have happened if George learned the letters on the computer or on a video? Would George have learned the letters if the man had only taught the words? Why? How did you learn the alphabet and how to read?

VI. Do you think the man taught George the right way to read? Why? Did the man let George be curious? Why? Is it important to read and write every day? Why?

Story Questions *(cont.)*

Curious George Goes to the Hospital

I.	What was George's problem? Why did the doctor take x-ray pictures? How was George's problem solved? What else happened at the hospital? What pictures were on the finished puzzle?
II.	Why did George eat the puzzle piece? What did the different doctors and nurses do to help George? How did George's curiosity in the playroom lead him to trouble? How did the mayor, doctors, nurses, and children react to the mess George made?
III.	What might have happened if George could have read the words on the big box? Do you think George might go back to the hospital again? Why? How might George have been if he was the only one in the children's ward and playroom?
IV.	How did George react to each new experience in the hospital? What effect did George have on Betsy and the other children in the hospital? What do you think George learned from this experience?
V.	Do you think the next time George will think before opening a strange box? Why? What might have happened if George had wheeled the go-cart out of the hospital? How might the story have changed if George had been in his own private room with only a television set?
VI.	If you were in the hospital, would you act like George did? Why? Do you think the children learned anything from George? Why? If you didn't feel well, would you want your parents to call the doctor right away? Why? Do you think the hospital director will want George to return to the hospital? Why?

Stick Puppet Theaters

Make a class set of puppet theaters (one for each student), or make one theater for every two to four students. The patterns and directions for making the stick puppets are on page 19 and 20.

Materials

- 22" x 28" (56 cm x 71 cm) piece of colored poster board per theater

- markers, crayons, or paints

- scissors or a craft knife

Directions

1. Fold the poster board 8" (20 cm) in from each of the shorter sides. (See picture below.)

2. Cut a window in the front panel, large enough to accommodate two or three stick puppets.

3. Let the children personalize their own theaters using the markers, crayons, or paint.

4. Laminate the stick puppet theaters to make them more durable. You may wish to send the theaters home at the end of the year or save them to use year after year.

Suggestions for Using the Puppets and the Puppet Theaters

- Prepare the stick puppets, using the directions on page 19. Use the puppets and puppet theaters with the Readers Theater Script on pages 43 and 44. (Let small groups of students take turns reading the parts and using the stick puppets.)

- Use the stick puppets and theaters for the puppet show in the Culminating Activity described on page 10.

- Have the students create a different script using the puppets. If other characters are needed, have the students make their own puppets.

- Make new stick puppets to retell one of the other Curious George books.

Stick Puppet Patterns

Directions: Reproduce the patterns on tagboard, cardstock, or construction paper. Have students color the patterns. Cut along the dotted lines. To complete the stick puppets, glue each pattern to a tongue depressor or craft stick. Use the stick puppets with puppet theaters and/or the readers theater script on pages 43 and 44.

Curious George

Sailor

Man with the Big, Yellow Hat

Stick Puppet Patterns *(cont.)*

See page 19 for directions.

Policeman

Fireman

Balloon Man

A Story Retell

George did many curious things in the book, *Curious George*. First, read the sentences telling about his adventures. Second, number them in order, the way they happened in the story. Third, read them in order to retell the story.

☐ George escaped from the prison through an open door.

☐ Then the man took George to the Zoo, and George was happy.

☐ George held onto a bunch of balloons that took him high over the city.

☐ By mistake, George called the fire station on the telephone.

☐ George was caught by a man with a big, yellow hat and taken to a big ship.

☐ The man with the big, yellow hat found him and paid the balloon man for all the balloons.

☐ George was a curious monkey who lived in Africa.

☐ The firemen put George in prison where he could stay out of trouble.

☐ George went to live in the city with the man with the big, yellow hat.

☐ The sailors rescued George when he fell into the water.

 Be Curious!

What do you do in one day? Write, in sequence, what you do in one day, beginning with when you get out of bed in the morning to when you go to sleep in the evening.

Curious George or Bored George?

George is very curious. To be curious is to be interested in many things. George was never bored. To be bored means not to be interested in anything. *Curious* and *bored* are opposites. **Antonyms** are words that are opposites. *Curious* and *interested* are words that have the same meaning and are called **synonyms**.

Draw lines to match the words that are *antonyms*.

happy	mean
bad	sad
kind	quiet
noisy	healthy
sick	cold
hot	good

Write a sentence using two of these antonyms.

_____

Draw lines to match the words that are *synonyms*.

happy	nice
bad	loud
kind	awful
noisy	ill
sick	burning
hot	glad

Write a sentence using two of these synonyms.

_____

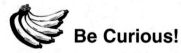 **Be Curious!**

Write a question. Then have a friend write the answer.

Did You Ever Wonder?

George wondered how sea gulls could fly, so he tried to fly. That's when he ended up in the water. Have you ever wondered about something you have seen, heard, smelled, touched, or tasted? Write a story about something you have wondered about.

_____

(title)

_____

_____

_____

_____

_____

_____

_____

_____

 Be Curious!

Ask your best friend to share with you a time when he or she wondered about something. Then, on paper, write about what happened.

Rhymes Make Sense!

Rhymes are words that have the same ending sounds, like *George* and *gorge*. All living beings have five senses: *hearing*, *sight*, *smell*, *taste*, and *touch*. These senses help us learn about where we live.

Read the sense rhymes about Curious George. Then write the words that rhyme and the sense for each rhyme.

	Rhyming Words	**Sense**

1. Curious George, Curious George, _____ _____
   Is the cutest monkey I ever did see. _____
   He likes to climb the banana tree _____
   And eat lots of bananas for free.

2. Curious George, Curious George, _____ _____
   Is the noisiest monkey I ever did hear. _____
   He likes to chatter in my ear, _____
   And you can hear him far and near.

3. Curious George, Curious George, _____ _____
   Is the softest monkey I ever did touch. _____
   He likes to hug me very much. _____
   And when he does, it is such
   A furry, furry feeling!

4. Curious George, Curious George, _____ _____
   Has many things that he likes to taste. _____
   His favorite is his monkey toothpaste. _____
   That, you'll be sure, he will not waste.

5. Curious George, Curious George, _____ _____
   Has many things he likes to smell, _____
   And some are even inside of a shell. _____
   They make him feel, oh so very well.

Be Curious!

Use rhyming words and write a sense rhyme about yourself or someone else.

A New Curious George Tale!

"This is George." These are the words in the first sentences that begin each of the first seven Curious George books. They tell whom the story is about.

The second sentences in the books tell where George lived. These sentences are different. For example, "He lived in Africa," or "He lived with his friend, the man with the yellow hat."

The third sentences in the books tell more about George. These sentences are different. For example, "He was a good little monkey and always very curious," or "George is a little monkey, and all monkeys are curious."

Now, it is your turn to write a new beginning to a Curious George book. Write three sentences to begin the book. The first sentence tells who the story is about—George. The second sentence tells where he lived. The third sentence tells more about George.

_____

_____

_____

_____

_____

_____

_____

_____

_____

_____

 **Be Curious!**

Now, add more sentences and finish the story about George.

Two or Three Syllables?

Did you know that there are only three words with more than two syllables in *Curious George Flies a Kite?* A **syllable** is a part of a word that is said in one sound, like *mon* in monkey. Monkey has two syllables—*mon* and *key*. In the word search below, there are fifteen words. Find the two-syllable words and color them yellow. Color the words with more than two syllables red. The words go up, down, across, and diagonally.

The words are as follows:

- another
- away
- baby
- bunny
- curious

- funny
- garden
- happy
- helicopter
- into

- little
- monkey
- shouted
- window
- yellow

A	S	W	B	H	A	P	P	Y	A
N	H	I	U	V	B	A	B	Y	W
O	O	N	N	I	N	T	O	J	A
T	U	D	N	K	W	C	D	Z	Y
H	T	O	Y	O	F	U	N	N	Y
E	E	W	L	M	O	N	K	E	Y
R	D	L	D	G	A	R	D	E	N
G	E	X	C	U	R	I	O	U	S
Y	L	I	T	T	L	E	Q	A	Z
H	E	L	I	C	O	P	T	E	R

 **Be Curious!**

Read *Curious George Flies a Kite* and find the fifteen words in the word search.

A Bunch of Balloons!

George was curious when he saw the balloon man with the red, green, blue, and yellow balloons. He wanted a red balloon. Solve the addition and subtraction problems in the balloons. Then color the balloons with these answers:

431 = red   92 = green   715 = blue   37 = yellow

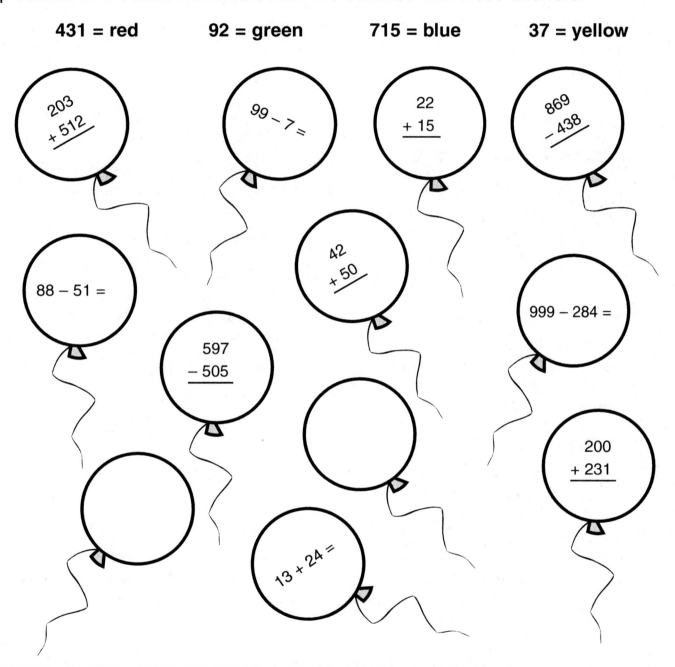

Be Curious!

Two balloons do not have a problem. Write an addition or subtraction problem in each balloon, so there are three balloons of each color in the bunch.

Fire Trucks, Fire Engines

A fire engine is a truck that has equipment such as hoses, ladders, and pumps to put out fires. Pumps are used to move water through a hose to put out a fire. Ladders are used to rescue people and animals trapped in high places.

Read about the different cars and trucks that can be seen in a fire station and then answer the questions.

Pumper Engine

It goes to all fires. It has many hoses. It pumps water from a hydrant through its hoses. It has 2 tires in the front and 4 tires in the back. How many tires in all?

———

Tanker Truck

It hauls water that is used to fight fires. It has 2 tires in the front and 4 tires in the back. How many tires in all?_____

Snorkel Truck

It has a basket-like cage where firefighters stand. It can be raised and moved around to fight fires in tall buildings. It has 2 tires in the front and 8 tires in the back. How many tires in all?_____

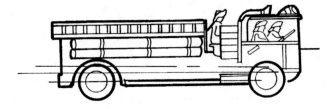

Ladder Truck

It has ladders to rescue people in high places. It has 2 tires in the front and 8 tires in the back. How many tires in all?_____

Rescue Fire Truck

It carries injured people to the hospital. It has 2 tires in the front and 4 tires on the back. How many tires in all?_____

Fire Chief's Car

The fire chief drives the car to fires. It has 2 tires in the front and 2 tires in the back. How many tires in all?_____

 Be Curious!

Look at different kinds of trucks and count how many tires are on each of them. Were all the numbers even? What would happen if a truck had an odd number of tires?

Telephones

Where would we be without telephones? Telephones are used for sending and receiving messages. George watched his friend telephone the zoo. Then he wanted to try the telephone, too. He dialed the fire station, which was an emergency call. Most emergency calls are dialed 911, and only dial that number if it is a real emergency. You know what happened to Curious George!

Solve and write about how you solved these word problems that use telephone numbers.

1. Geno's phone number is 524–4518. What is the sum of these digits?

   _____

   How did you solve the problem? _____

   _____

2. Tiana's phone number is 123–4567. What is the sum of these digits?

   _____

   How did you solve the problem? _____

   _____

3. What is the difference between the sums of Geno's and Tiana's phone numbers? _____ How did you solve the problem? _____

   _____

4. Hanna's area code is 582. Diablo's area code is 340. What is the sum of their area codes? _____ How did you solve the problem? _____
   _____ What is their difference? _____
   How did you solve the problem? _____

   _____

 Be Curious!

What is your telephone number, and what is the telephone number of your favorite friend or favorite relative?

Pasta, Pasta in the Pot!

George was curious about what was in the big pot in the kitchen at the restaurant. Of course, it was spaghetti! Spaghetti is a type of pasta. Pasta is a kind of dough made from flour and water. George ate the pasta, but he also had to clean up the kitchen.

Read and solve the time word problems about his visit to the restaurant. Then show the times in your answers on the clocks.

1. In the city, at 10:00, George walked into the kitchen. Five minutes later he found the spaghetti pot. What time was it?
   _____

2. At 10:05 he began eating the spaghetti. Ten minutes later he had eaten five yards of spaghetti. What time was it?
   _____

3. He was still hungry, so he ate 5 more yards of spaghetti in 10 minutes. Then what time was it? _____

4. At 10:25 the cook came into the kitchen. It took him ten more minutes to unwrap the spaghetti wrapped around George. What time was it? _____

5. Then the cook told George to clean up the kitchen. George cleaned it in five minutes. What time was it when he finished? _____

6. At 10:40 George began to wash the dishes, two at a time. He washed 50 dishes in five minutes! What time was it then? _____

7. For how many minutes was George busy in the kitchen? _____

 Be Curious!

Keep a journal that tells how long it takes you to do different jobs and activities.

Let's Follow George!

It would be fun to follow Curious George and have many exciting adventures! Now, it's your turn to do this! Sing this song to the tune of "Mary Had a Little Lamb" and fill in the blanks to tell where you went with George and what happened.

There once was a little monkey named George,

A monkey named George, a monkey named George.

The once was a little monkey named George,

And he was always curious.

Everywhere that Curious George went,

Curious George went, Curious George went,

Everywhere that Curious George went,

We followed him there, too.

We followed him to the _____,

To the _____ , to the_____.

We followed him to the _____,

And we saw lots of _____.

We followed him to the _____,

To the _____ , to the _____.

We followed him to the _____,

And we heard lots of _____.

(*continued on page 32*)

Let's Follow George! *(cont.)*

We followed him to the _____,

To the _____, to the _____.

We followed him to the _____,

And we smelled lots of _____.

We followed him to the _____,

To the _____ , to the _____.

We followed him to the _____,

And we tasted lots of _____.

We followed him to the _____,

To the _____, to the _____.

We followed him to the _____,

And we touched lots of _____.

We're so happy we followed George,

Followed George, followed George.

We're so happy we followed George,

'Cause we had lots of fun.

 Be Curious!

Write this song again using your name instead of George's, and sing about where you would like to go.

The Seven Continents

George was a monkey who lived in Africa. Africa is one of the seven continents in the world. A continent is a large area of land. On the map of the world, draw a line from each continent to its name below the map. Then color the continents the appropriate colors.

Africa = green   Antarctica = yellow   Asia = brown   Australia = purple

Europe = orange   North America = red   South America = pink

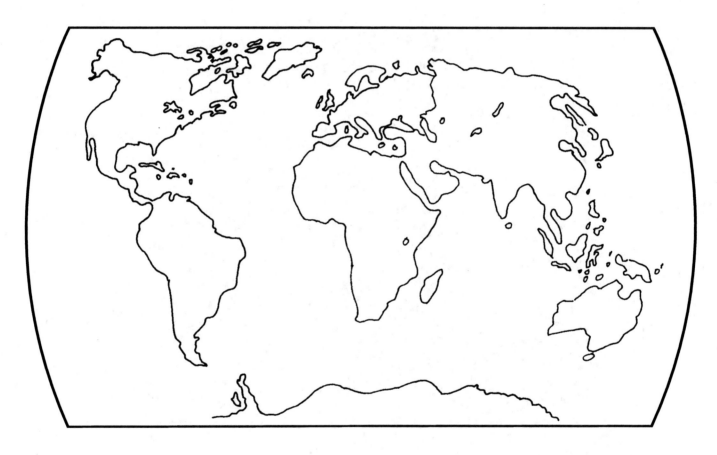

Africa   Antarctica   Asia

         Australia   Europe

North America   South America

 Be Curious!

George went across the ocean from Africa in a big ship. To what continent do you think the man with the big, yellow hat took him? Why?

Curious George's Bicycle

The man with the yellow hat gave George a bicycle. A bicycle is a vehicle with two wheels, and it has many different parts. Below is a drawing of George's bicycle. It has several different parts. Write the names listed below on the lines next to the parts on the bicycle. Then, share with a partner why each of these parts is important for George when he rides his bike.

The parts are listed as follows:

- seat
- handlebars
- headlight
- tire
- chain
- pedal
- parking stand
- rear reflector

 Be Curious!

Draw a picture of a bicycle of today and compare it to George's simple bicycle. How are they the same? How are they different?

Let's Transport Curious George

How can Curious George go from one place to another, besides using his two legs and feet and his two arms and hands? Read the riddles, and from the word list, write the vehicle's name that he could use. Your answer should rhyme with a word or words in the riddle.

Word List

airplane   bicycle   bus   car   motorcycle   train   truck   van   wagon

---

1. I am large and have lots of seats. I can carry many passengers without a fuss.

   What am I? _____

2. I have two wheels, no motor, and handlebars for steering. Sometimes I can stop on a nickel.

   What am I? _____

3. You probably ride in me every day, either to school or somewhere to play. I can go near or far.

   What am I? _____

4. I am larger than a car and can carry more near or far. Nan, Stan, and Fran love to ride in a

   _____.

5. I many have 18 wheels and can be very large. I carry lots of things and hardly ever get stuck.

   I am a _____.

6. I have wings, and I can fly. I can be small or very big. Sometimes I fly through a hurricane.

   I am an _____.

 Be Curious!

How many vehicles can you name? Make a list of vehicles, and tell how they are alike and different.

No Smoking, Please!

George's friend with the yellow hat smoked a pipe, so George tried it, too. Tobacco is put into a pipe and smoked. Tobacco is a plant from which the leaves are dried and chopped, then lighted and used for smoking. Tobacco is dangerous for your health. It can cause heart and lung disease and cancer in the body. Cancer is a disease in which some cells in the body grow quickly and destroy the healthy part of the body.

Help others not to smoke. Create a sign that tells people not to smoke. Make copies of your sign and give them to your friends.

_____
(title)

_____

_____

_____

_____

_____

_____

 Be Curious!

Choose something that is good for your health, find out more about it, and make a card that tells why it is good for you.

Bananas! Bananas!

Why does George like to eat bananas? Read this story to learn more about bananas. Then write about what you learned about bananas, and why you should eat them.

Bananas

Bananas are a healthy food to eat and easy to digest. They have many vitamins. Vitamins are things in food that are important for good health. They have lots of vitamin A, which helps to keep the skin and body healthy. Bananas have vitamin B that makes the red blood cells strong and vitamin C that keeps the organs of the body healthy. Bananas are also full of potassium that helps keep muscles healthy and strong. Now you know why George likes to eat bananas! Bananas are good for everyone!

_____

_____

_____

_____

_____

_____

_____

_____

 Be Curious!

Are all bananas yellow? What is a Hawaiian Red? A Blue Java? A Plaintain?

Fruit! Fruit!

George likes to eat bananas. A banana is a fruit that grows on tall plants that look like trees. A fruit is the part of a plant that grows from its flowers, and the fruit has the plant's seeds. In most parts of the world, fruit grows on bushes, plants, trees, or vines.

Write the names of fruit that grow on bushes, plants, trees, and vines in the boxes below.

bushes	trees

plants	vines

 Be Curious!

Try new fruits you have never tasted before. Do they have seeds? Where are they grown? Did you like them? Why or why not?

Sam, Miss Sam, Ham, and George: Famous Monkeynauts!

Monkeys are like human beings and can use their hands well. That is why they were often used in space experiments before humans went into space. Read the facts about Sam, Miss Sam, and Ham, famous monkeys from the U.S.A. who went into space in a space capsule. A space capsule is the part of the spacecraft in which the monkeys traveled.

Sam

He went into space in 1959. His flight was to test equipment. He went up about 55 miles into space. His trip was about two hours. A ship recovered him in the Atlantic Ocean.

Ham

He went into space in 1961. His flight was to test how the capsule could work in space. He went about 108 miles into space. He was recovered in the Atlantic Ocean. When he returned, he ate an apple.

Miss Sam

She went into space in 1960. Her flight was to test the escape system. She went up about 9 miles into space. A helicopter recovered her in the Atlantic Ocean.

George

 Be Curious!

Find out more about animals that have gone into space by researching on the Internet.

George, a Famous Monkeynaut!

George, too, was asked to go into space, because he was a "bright" monkey and could do "all sorts of things." Read about his trip in *Curious George Gets a Medal*. Then write a summary about his trip into space in the space capsule.

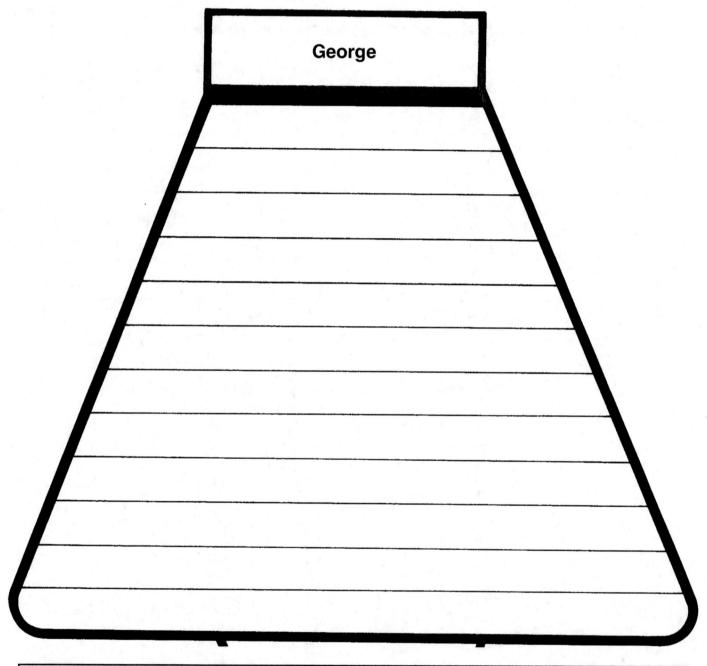

George

 Be Curious!

Pretend you are an astronaut going into space and write a summary about your trip.

Hats and Caps

George met a man with a large, yellow, straw hat. George was curious and decided to put the hat on his head. Then he was caught!

Draw a picture of your favorite hat or cap. Then write a paragraph about it.

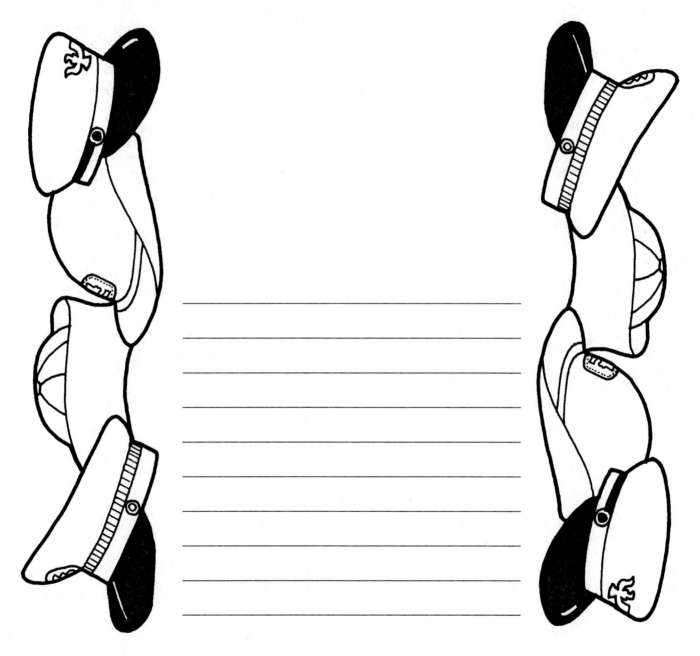

_____

_____

_____

_____

_____

_____

_____

_____

 Be Curious!

Read and talk about the labels and words on different hats and caps.
What do the words and numbers mean?

Letter Pictures

The man with the yellow hat taught George how to make the letters of the alphabet. He first wrote the letter and then drew a picture around each letter. The letter X could become a picture of George dangling from a tree!

There are four different letters in the name George. In each square, draw either the uppercase or lowercase letter and create a picture around the letter.

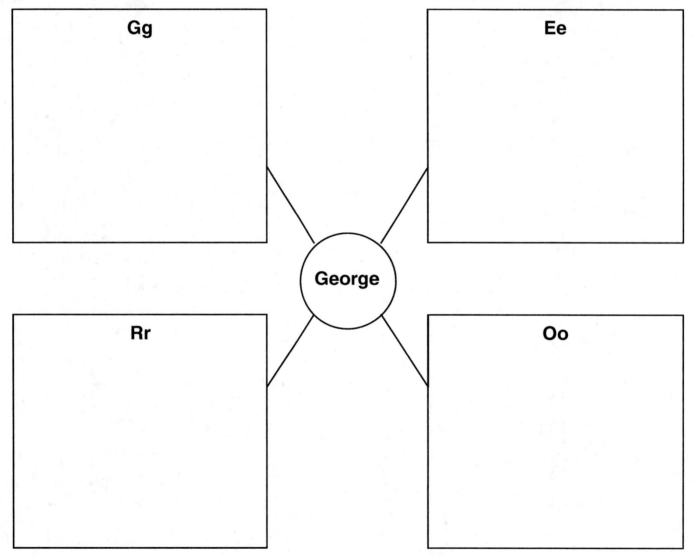

Gg

Ee

George

Rr

Oo

 Be Curious!

Take the letters in your name and create a new letter picture with each letter.

Readers Theater Script

Characters:	George, Fireman, Balloon Man, Policeman, Sailor, Narrator 1, Narrator 2

Narrator 1:   This story is about George. He lived with his friend, the man with the yellow hat. He was a good little monkey, but always curious.

Narrator 2:   One day George read about a contest. The words said "Be Who You Would Like To Be! Choose a character you would like to be, and then write in 50 words or less why you would like to be that character."

Narrator 1:   The winner's ideas would be published in a book, and the winner would get $100. You could enter as many times as you wanted.

George: This sounds like a great contest! I wonder what it would be like to be a fireman?

Narrator 2:   George became more curious and began to imagine himself as a fireman.

George: Ahhh! Ahhh! Ahhh! I am Fred the fireman! I think I'll ask a fireman how I should act.

Fireman: I am a fireman, and I am not a real animal. I like to put out fires! Sometimes I help people, and sometimes I am in dangerous places! Ahhh! Ahhh! Ahhh! I love being a fireman!

George: Ahhh! Ahhh! Ahhh! Okay. Maybe I'd like to be a balloon man.

Narrator 1:   George became more curious and began to imagine himself as a balloon man.

George: HA! HA! HA! I am Bob the balloon man! I think I'll ask a balloon man at the park how I should act.

Balloon Man: I am a balloon man, and I sell balloons to all the children who walk in the streets. I like to be silly and tell jokes, too. HA! HA! HA! I love being a balloon man!

Narrator 2:   George became more curious and began to imagine himself as a sailor.

Readers Theater Script *(cont.)*

George: AHOY! AHOY! AHOY! I am Sammy the sailor! I think I'll ask the sailor by the ship how I should act.

Sailor: I am a sailor, and I work on a big ship! I sail on the ocean. AHOY! AHOY! AHOY! I love being a sailor!

George: AHOY! AHOY! AHOY! Maybe I'd like to be a policeman!

Narrator 1:   George became more curious and began to imagine himself as a policeman.

George: ERRR! ERRR! ERRR! There goes the siren! I am Pete the policeman, and I think I'll ask a policeman how I should act.

Policeman: I am one of many policemen, and I am a real person. Police carry out the law and help to stop crime. My job can be dangerous, and I have to be very brave. ERRR! ERRR! ERRR! I love being a policeman!

Narrator 2:   So this is what George wrote:

George: Well, I think I'd like to be me. I am a monkey, and monkeys are real! I am a mammal, and I am very smart. I can move through trees, and I love bananas! Monkeys live together in groups and have fun with each other. I love being a monkey! From, George

Narrator 1:   George entered the contest on time and wrote about his ideas in just 50 words! He was chosen the winner!

Narrator 2:   He got $100 and was curious how to share the money with the fireman, balloon man, sailor, and policeman, because they helped him to pick himself as the character.

Narrator 1:   So, he gave each friend $20 and kept $20 for himself. George was very happy!

Narrator 2:   So, everybody give three loud cheers for C-U-R-I-O-U-S G-E-O-R-G-E!

              (Everybody cheers, "Curious George! Curious George! Curious George!")

Bibliography

Curious George and the Bunny. Rey, Margret. Houghton Mifflin, 1998.

Curious George and the Dinosaur. Rey, Margret. Houghton Mifflin, 1989.

Curious George and the Hot Air Balloon. Rey, Margret. Houghton Mifflin, 1998.

Curious George and the Pizza. Rey, Margret. Houghton Mifflin, 1985.

Curious George and the Puppies. Rey, Margret. Houghton Mifflin, 1998.

Curious George and the Fire Station. Ed. by Rey, Margret. Houghton Mifflin, 1985.

Curious George Flies a Kite. Rey, Margret and H. A. Rey. Houghton Mifflin, 1958.

Curious George Feeds the Animals. Rey, Margret. Houghton Mifflin, 1998.

Curious George Gets a Medal. Rey, H. A. Houghton Mifflin, 1957.

Curious George Goes to the Chocolate Factory. Rey, Margret. Houghton Mifflin, 1998.

Curious George Goes to the Hospital. Rey, Margret and H. A. Rey. Houghton Mifflin, 1966.

Curious George Goes to a Movie. Rey, Margret. Houghton Mifflin, 1998.

Curious George Goes to a Restaurant. Rey, Margret and Allan J. Shalleck. Houghton Mifflin, 1998.

Curious George Goes to an Ice Cream Shop. Rey, Margret and Allan J. Shalleck. Houghton Mifflin, 1989.

Curious George Goes to School. Rey, Margret and Allan J. Shalleck. Houghton Mifflin, 1989.

Curious George Goes to the Aquarium. Ed. by Rey, Margret. Houghton Mifflin, 1984.

Curious George Goes to the Dentist. Rey, Margret and Allan J. Shalleck. Houghton Mifflin, 1989.

Curious George in the Snow. Rey, Margret. Houghton Mifflin, 1998.

Curious George Learns the Alphabet. Rey, H. A. Houghton Mifflin, 1963.

Curious George Makes Pancakes. Rey, Margret. Houghton Mifflin, 1998.

Curious George Plays Baseball. Rey, Margret and Allan J. Shalleck. Houghton Mifflin, 1986.

Curious George Rides a Bike. Rey, H. A. Houghton Mifflin, 1952.

Curious George Takes a Job. Rey, H. A. Houghton Mifflin, 1941.

Curious George's Dream. Rey, Margret. Houghton Mifflin, 1998.

Curious George's Opposites. Rey, Margret. Houghton Mifflin, 1998.

Activities for Other Curious George Books

The following is a list of suggested activities for the other six original Curious George books.

Curious George Takes a Job

1. Complete the Pasta, Pasta in the Pot! activity on page 30.
2. Complete the Let's Transport Curious George activity on page 35.
3. Research animals that live in a zoo. Use the information to make a zoo-animal book.
4. Compare and contrast country and city life. A Venn diagram may be used to write and display the information.
5. Read and share restaurant menus. Create meal orders and their costs.
6. Learn more about different kinds of pasta and pasta recipes. Combine the recipes into a pasta recipe book.
7. Pretend you are George and you have four hands. You can wash dishes twice as quickly. Create dishwashing and drying word problems, multiplying by two.
8. Research job skills required for different careers. Choose a career and write a report about it.

Curious George Rides a Bike

1. Curious George was brought three years ago from the jungle to the home of the man in the yellow hat. Write about what you did three years ago.
2. Complete Curious George's Bicycle on page 34.
3. Design a new bicycle.
4. Create new shapes from folded paper. Some examples include airplanes, hats, origami, etc.
5. Find a different way to recycle newspaper and have a Recycling Fair to share your ideas.
6. Research the ostrich—will it eat anything?
7. Brainstorm a list of behavior rules and the consequences, if broken.
8. Discuss different emergencies and how to react to them.
9. Create math word problems about delivering newspapers.

Curious George Gets a Medal

1. Complete Sam, Miss Sam, Ham, and George: Famous Monkeynauts! on page 39.
2. Complete George, a Famous Monkeynaut! on page 40.
3. Write a letter or an e-mail message to someone.
4. Explore and experiment with different kinds of ink and the ways to absorb the ink.
5. Compare soaps of the past (powders) and soaps of today (liquids, cremes, etc.).
6. Research different kinds of pumps and their functions. Some examples include water pumps, bike pumps, etc.
7. Compare museums and zoos and how they are alike and different. For example, compare extinct animals (dinosaurs) and living animals (zoo animals).
8. Design a medal as a reward for an accomplishment.
9. Pick a dinosaur. Write a report describing it and include a picture.

Activities for Other Curious George Books *(cont.)*

Curious George Flies a Kite

1. Complete Two or Three Syllables? on page 26.
2. George helped Bill rescue his kite. Write about a time when you helped someone.
3. Brainstorm a list of different kinds of aircraft. Make an aircraft book including information and pictures about each aircraft.
4. Create fishing math word problems that might include the length and weight of fish, number of fish caught, number of fish that got away, etc.
5. Design a chart showing different kinds of fish and their characteristics.
6. George liked to look out of the big window. Design different windows that may be seen in different kinds of buildings. Some examples include an igloo, hotel, jail, church, etc.
7. Create a new "Get the Bunny" game. Write the directions in sequence and then play the game.
8. Make simple paper kites and then fly them. Discuss the experience and how the kites flew.

Curious George Learns the Alphabet

1. Complete the Letter Pictures on page 42.
2. Write and illustrate an ABC Tongue Twister Book using some of the words in the book. Some examples include the following: "An alligator ate an apple," or "A busy bee bit Bill."
3. Observe the number of legs on the different animals in the book (2, 4, 6, 8, etc.) and create a graph to show the number of animals with different numbers of legs.
4. Display lists of different letters and create words using the letters. Some examples include the following: (a, b, c = cab), (a, b, c, d, e, f, g = bag, cage, bed, bad), etc.
5. Draw a picture using the letters of your name.
6. George liked to play football. Write about your favorite game.
7. Write the uppercase and lowercase manuscript letters that look alike, except for size. Some examples are V, v; W, w; Z, z; etc.
8. One dozen equals 12. "A baker's dozen" equals 13. Write the addition- and subtraction-fact families for 12 and 13.

Curious George Goes to the Hospital

1. Read and perform the Readers Theater Script on pages 43 and 44, with puppets. (See pages 18, 19, and 20.)
2. A jigsaw puzzle is a wooden or cardboard puzzle with pieces that fit together. Create a picture on card stock or heavy tagboard. Cut apart into pieces to form a jigsaw puzzle.
3. Jigsaw is a compound word. Brainstorm lists of compound words and illustrate them.
4. Discuss and stress the importance of putting only "food" in your mouth.
5. Become familiar with medical terms used in the book. Some examples include *stethoscope, x-ray, barium, blood transfusion, temperature, blood pressure, shots, pills,* etc.
6. Design a new "go-cart" or "wheelchair."
7. George helped many people to laugh. Write a story about what makes you laugh.
8. George wore an identification bracelet in the hospital. Create a bracelet that includes your full name and address.
9. When all seven books have been read, complete A New Curious George Tale! on page 25.

Answer Key

Page 21

1. George was a curious monkey who lived in Africa.
2. George was caught by a man with a big, yellow hat and taken to a big ship.
3. The sailors rescued George when he fell into the water.
4. George went to live in the city with the man with the big, yellow hat.
5. By mistake, George called the fire station on the telephone.
6. The firemen put George in prison where he could stay out of trouble.
7. George escaped from the prison through an open door.
8. George held onto a bunch of balloons that took him high over the city.
9. The man with the big, yellow hat found him and paid the balloon man for all the balloons.
10. Then the man took George to the Zoo, and George was happy.

Page 22

Antonyms

happy—sad
bad—good
kind—mean
noisy—quiet
sick—healthy
hot—cold

Synonyms

happy—glad
bad—awful
kind—nice
noisy—loud
sick—ill
hot—burning

Page 24

1. see, tree, free
   sight
2. hear, ear, near
   hearing
3. touch, much, such
   touch
4. taste, toothpaste, waste
   taste
5. smell, shell, well
   smell

Page 26

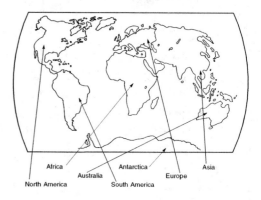

yellow words = away, baby, bunny, funny, garden, happy, into, little, monkey, shouted, window, yellow

red words = another, curious, helicopter

Page 27

203 + 512 = 715 (blue)

99 – 7 = 92 (green)

22 +15 = 37 (yellow)

869 – 438 = 431 (red)

88 – 51 = 37 (yellow)

597 – 505 = 92 (green)

42 + 50 = 92 (green)

999 – 284 = 715 (blue)

13 + 24 = 37 (yellow)

200 + 231 = 431 (red)

Page 28

Pumper Engine—6 tires

Tanker Truck—6 tires

Snorkel Truck—10 tires

Ladder Truck—10 tires

Rescue Fire Truck—6 tires

Fire Chief's Car—4 tires

Page 29

1. 29
   5 + 2 + 4 + 4 + 5 + 1 + 8 = 29
2. 28
   1 + 2 + 3 + 4 + 5 + 6 + 7 = 28
3. 1
   29 – 28 = 1
4. 922
   582 + 340 = 922
   242
   582 – 340 = 242

Page 30

1. 10:05
2. 10:15
3. 10:25
4. 10:35
5. 10:40
6. 10:45
7. 45 minutes

Page 33

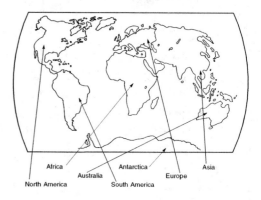

Page 34

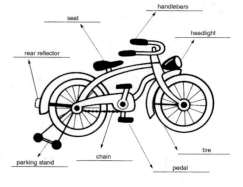

Page 35

1. bus
2. bicycle
3. car
4. van
5. truck
6. airplane